Given to
THE FARMINGTON LIBRARY
of
FARMINGTON, CONNECTICUT

IN MEMORY OF

LAURA VIOLETTE

BY

Mr. and Mrs. Donald C. Martin

DISCARD

P9-DMV-872

Love Letters

Arnold Adoff
illustrated by Lisa Desimini

THE BLUE SKY PRESS

An Imprint of Scholastic Inc. · New York

Farmington Library
Farmington, CT 06032

J
811.54
ADO

THE BLUE SKY PRESS

Text copyright © 1997 by Arnold Adoff
Illustrations copyright © 1997 by Lisa Desimini

All rights reserved.
No part of this publication may be reproduced or stored
in a retrieval system or transmitted in any form or by any
means, electronic, mechanical, photocopying, recording,
or otherwise, without written permission of the publisher.

For information regarding permission, please write to:
Permissions Department,
The Blue Sky Press, an imprint of Scholastic Inc.,
555 Broadway, New York, New York 10012.

The Blue Sky Press is a registered trademark of Scholastic Inc.

Special thanks to Hasbro, Inc. for the use of MR. POTATO HEAD®.
MR. POTATO HEAD® is a trademark of Hasbro, Inc.
All rights reserved.

Library of Congress Cataloging-in-Publication Data
Adoff, Arnold.
Love letters / Arnold Adoff; illustrated by Lisa Desimini.
p.   cm.
Summary: A collection of twenty poems written by kids and klutzes,
secret admirers and detractors, friends, enemies, and skeptics
to the objects of their affection—or aversion.

ISBN 0-590-48478-8
1. Love-letters—Juvenile poetry.   2. Children's poetry, American.
[1. Love—Poetry.   2. American poetry.]   I. Desimini, Lisa, ill.
II. Title   PS3551.D66L68   1997
811'.54—dc20   96-19982   CIP AC

12 11 10 9 8 7 6 5 4 3 2 1   7 8 9/9 0/0
Printed in the United States of America   36
First printing, January 1997

Production supervision by Angela Biola
Art direction by Kathleen Westray
Designed by Kristina Iulo

Dear Ginger Belle:
These Love Letters,
These Love Poems
Are
For
You
For All The Days
Of All The Years.

Your Own Arn.

For Matt
L.D.

Dear Ms. Back Row:

I t h i n k
I like you
     a lot, especially
          since
         Christmas
when you wore that angel
crown on top of your so
f l u f f y brown h a i r.
Just
smile
at me
o n e
t i m e
on your way past my desk.

Yours: First Seat First Row.

Gg Hh Ii Jj Kk Ll Mm Nn Oo Pp Qq Rr Ss Tt Uu

$4 - 2 = 2$

$=$

$2 + 0 = 2$

$2 \div \dfrac{1}{2} = 2$

$\dfrac{2}{50 \,/\, 100}$

Dear New Boy:

at   the
blackboard
just
arrived in
town with
           all
           the
           answers.
Can you see
that
one
plus
one equals
the
sum of you
and   who?

Your Only Correct Answer:
           O n l y M e.

Dear Playground Snow Girl:

I'll love you until
my nose falls off,
            until
my toes freeze
            inside
                my
            sneaks,
                until
m y m o u t h
goes s o u t h in
                the
            winter wind.
I'm waving
my fingers
        inside
        warm
        mittens.   Please
                wave
                b a c k.

Your Frozen Friend:
Frosty The Snow Boy.

Dear Playground Snow Boy:

Sorry you are frosty
                    frozen.
Now
watch my hand wave
                    you
                        far
            a w a y
from me
and my playing friends.
M a y b e
t o m o r r o w.
M a y b e not.
I love to run
when it's hot
        or cold,
    but I always
                    run
a l o n e.

Your Not-Yet Friend:
I c i c l e E y e s.

Dear Teacher:

I
hope
you never
find out
this red
h e a r t
is
from me.
I
like
to   stay
q u i e t
in
the
    class
    crowd.

Yours As A Mouse.

Dear Mrs. Nicely:

I love you more than
p e a n u t
b u t t e r s, more than
chocolate
c h i p s.
I love you more than
E l m e r
F u d d y
s t u t t e r s, more than
Shamu
f l i p s.
f
l
i
p
s.

Your Secret Student.

Dear
Mrs.
McNasty:

I
almost
like
you
today.

Your
Valentine
Avenger.

Dear Slick:

I love my
mom ma and my pop pa,
            and my gerbils,
            and
            one hamster,
and
my good dog,
and macaroni and cheese,
and my mountain trail
                    bike.
But
I'd leave them all
to shoot baskets
with you on even
the coldest
after
school
afternoon.

Yours: The Dribbler.

Dear Tall Girl At Front Table:

I love you more than peanut butter cookies
                                        crumble.
I love you more than yellow b e e s b u m b l e.
I also you more than dark thunder c l o u d s
  love
                                        r u m b l e.
I especially
  love
          you more than
me
m u m b l i n g
e x c u s e
me
after
I stumbled all over you   itwasanaccident,
as I walked up to get help
on Tuesday's math problem.

Your Future Friend: Big Foot.

Dear Fill-In-Your-Own-Name:

Please
excuse this printed valentine
but
I really do like at least ten
girls in our grade and maybe
                          a
                                 few m o r e,
and
my dad has this excellent c o p y
                                       i
                                       n
                                       g
                          machine

in his office.

Your Special Love:
Mr. One-And-Only.

Dear Gram:

I
very
much
love
your sugar cookies
and chocolate fudge.
B u t
I am
even
f u l l of love
when all your
j a r s
a r e e m p t y.

Your Grandson: Big Belly.

Dear Mom:

First: K e e p   m o m m i n g.
Second:
           I'm really thanking you.
Third: I'm s e r i o u s.
Fourth:
           Don't laugh.
Fifth: Please kiss
                   only
                        on
                             the
                  c h e e k.

Your Big Son: The Kid   Himself.

Dear Hard Working Dad:

Even when you snore
on the couch, I am
proud
with
     a
full
heart for
          you.

Your Son With Earplugs.

Dear Little Sis:

Here is a lesson for you:
   even though   these
               scissors
are supposed to be for
             us
             kids,
I did cut my finger
on the sharp edges
cutting out this heart
            for
            you.
P.S. #1:
Please
notice: the two drops
        ofmyblood,
                         yuch,
next to your name
on the front of this
            card.
P.S. #2:
The messy white paste-looking lumps
are only lumps of messy white paste.

Your Big Broth.

Dear Older Brother:

My list of reasons:

1. You were here first.
2. You will always be older than me.
3. I love you when
       you listen
       and don't
       h i t.

Your B e s t Brother: Peace.

Dear
Self:

How
a r e
y o u?
How
am
I?
I
am
fine.
Fine
I
am: because
I
am
my number
one
valentine.

Your
First
Love.

Dear Old Cat:

Under
the
bed:
your tail
s w i n g s
s o
s l o w l y
this
Monday
morning
before
s c h o o l.
We'll   play
        this
afternoon.

Your Sleepy Head Girl.

Dear
Dog
Spot:

I
love
you
this
special
day
and
for
ever.

Your Best Play Pal:
The Biscuit Girl.

Dear Prince:

My hair is very short,
I don't live high up
at the top of s o m e
                c a s t l e ,
and I don't
n e e d the
r e s c u e .
Just
ride
your
blue
bike
down   m y
street   and ring the bell
        this S a t u r d a y.

We can
chase
those
dragons
to
gether.

Your Potential Princess.

Dear Once Upon A Time:

I
k n o w
we can
write
that
story
together
i f
we
just
put
our
heads:
ear
t o
ear,
our
faces:
eye
t o
eye.

Your Happy Ending.